BLIZZARD

The Ice-Harvesting Horse

PAGE PUBLISHING
Conneaut Lake, PA

First originally published by Page Publishing 2024

ISBN 979-8-88960-897-4 (pbk)
ISBN 979-8-88960-906-3 (digital)

Printed in the United States of America

BLIZZARD

The Ice-Harvesting Horse

Jeanine Faietta Eastman

A long time ago, during the years of the early 1900s, ice was harvested from the frozen waters of Highland Lake in Windham, Maine. Wow, Maine really is the coolest state. People from away think it's just great!

Have you ever wondered how families kept their food cold before they had refrigerators to plug in and use every day? Ice harvesting was the way!

Huge blocks of ice were cut from the frozen lake garden. Later, they were delivered to homes by a horse–drawn wagon. The ice blocks were placed inside wooden ice boxes where food was stored, assuring it would stay nice and cold. Freshly picked, chilled strawberries never get old.

ICE

When the lake air is crisp and cold, you can see your own breath! The ice men and ice women are ready for success. Blizzard wears his custom fur coat to keep him warm. He can make it through any storm.

Horse-drawn plows were used to clear the snow and cut the lines on the frozen lake. This helped the workers know exactly where to cut the blocks, using sharp saws to slice through the frozen lake. With Blizzard's help, it was a piece of cake.

The cold, glimmering ice blocks were floated to the lake shore, then stored in the icehouse, always frozen and clear. Packed in burlap and sawdust, the ice blocks last an entire year.

Blizzard loved working during the coldest harvest with all his human friends. He knows they depend on him to keep their food cold and fresh all year long. How else would they make ice cream when it's so hot in the summer? Without ice, that would be a bummer!

Neighbors helping neighbors, you surely would agree. This is why Maine truly is the way that life should be.

Blizzard's Story

STRAIGHT FROM THE HORSE'S MOUTH

Another freezing morning on the lakeshore. We need it bone-chillin' cold for the ice to be eighteen inches thick. Then it will be safe to cut through the lake floor.

My best buddy, Luke, will hook me up to my plow. I'll scrape the snow off the frozen crops. The blocks will be ready to cut! With the help of the ice men and ice women, we all work together until the day's end.

Wow! It sure is windy. My mane is all tangled and messed up in the frigid air. Oh well, lake hair, don't care. I have important work to tend to.

"Let's go, Luke! No more horsing around. We need to finish our harvest before the sun goes down."

"Whoa, hold your horses! Open water is skimmed over the frozen lake. It's too dangerous to work today. We can't get there from here anyway."

"Come on, Luke. Let's get back to shore! We need to give the workers a warning to keep off the lake until the open water is completely frozen. We will head up the road apiece, Luke, and get you home. A good night's rest is much needed. When the sun rises in the morning, we will put the frozen harvest to the test."

I'll keep watch out my barn window. None of my human or animal friends will wander out on the lake floor. No accidents on Blizzard's watch, that's for sure! The moon is in full bloom tonight, shining down on the glistening lake. What a sight! It's the very same moon my ancestors before me depended on for light, guiding our way since the very first night!

My warm fur coat and mane has been brushed. Spiked horseshoes fit on my hooves so nice, preventing me from slipping and falling on the ice. I ate a healthy breakfast of grain and hay. After all, it is the most important meal of the day.

The neighbor ladies sewed me the coziest quilt. Ah…the best kind of warmth under the big sky above is my wicked good quilt, made with love. Talented quilters, that's the truth, but there are so many other tasks these ladies can do. Hardworking, determined, and strong women on the ice and shore. We couldn't manage without them, that's for sure!

I am stoked to head down to the lakeshore! Frigid air and blue sky, who could ask for anything more? A perfect way to start the day. Wild horses couldn't drag me away!

The once-open water is now frozen. We are safe for the harvest to begin. Snow has been scraped off the frozen lake; the lines are all cut. Workers get ready and go bundle up! The wild north wind is howling today. Cover your nose, or you'll be watching icicles growing all the way down to your toes. Sharpen those saws and cut the frozen crops. Let's get the job done before the temperature drops.

My sidekick Luke floats the frozen blocks of ice to shore. Now off to the icehouse go the blocks from the frozen lake floor. What a sight to see, ice stacked up so high. Plenty for all our neighbors to get by. Frozen blocks of ice are such a treasure. Helping out with this year's harvest has been my pleasure!

We surely know that before we go, we need to clean up our mess—ice picks, saws, wood scraps, trash, and such. The lake waters have been so good to us! It is our promise to keep them clean and clear for generations through the years.

We must not forget our wildlife friends; this is their home too. Preserving the lake waters for all is the right thing to do.

    Today is the day we deliver ice blocks to Luke's family home. They are so proud and appreciate all the hard work he has done.

    Tomorrow is a school day for Luke. Do you know he walks two miles to school? Every day, uphill, both ways during snowstorms? It's true! Way to go, buddy. I am so proud of you!

ICE

ICE

The coldest harvest will return next season. Until then, my sidekick and I will deliver ice blocks to all our neighbors and friends, assuring them cold, fresh food until the year's end.

Ayuh, we will be tending to our frozen garden once again!

ABOUT THE AUTHOR

Jeanine was born and raised in the great state of Maine. She loves it so much she has never lived anyplace else! Living with her family on Highland Lake, she has cherished the fresh and frozen lake waters since childhood.

Jeanine fondly remembers her grandpa's stories of ice harvesting that took place on the lake during the early 1900s. She finds it fascinating that the frozen lake water provided such a valuable commodity to many local Maine families.

She believes it is important to tell the story of the frozen crops to younger generations so they would learn what life was like for those who came before them.

Jeanine hopes that all ages will love the story of Blizzard, the ice-harvesting horse, that Blizzard will make you smile, inspire you to help your neighbors, and maybe even have icicles growing from your nose all the way down to your toes! Blizzard shares his adventures straight from the horse's mouth.

This is Jeanine's second published children's book. Her first book, *The Very Same Moon*, is a story of the moon over a lake, guiding the way for all the neighbors and animal friends with its bright light. Look for the very same moon as it makes a special appearance in *Blizzard, the Ice-Harvesting Horse*.

www.ingramcontent.com/pod-product-compliance
Lightning Source LLC
Chambersburg PA
CBHW041821110726
48006CB00019B/2462